A Summary of the Laws of Massachusetts, Relative to the Settlement, Support, Employment and Removal of Paupers

by Jonathan Leavitt

Address:
HardPress
8345 NW 66TH ST #2561
MIAMI FL 33166-2626
USA
Email: info@hardpress.net

Leavitt

A
SUMMARY
OF THE
LAWS OF MASSACHUSETTS,
RELATIVE TO THE
SETTLEMENT, SUPPORT, EMPLOYMENT
AND
REMOVAL
OF
PAUPERS.

.. ..

By JONATHAN LEAVITT, Esq.
Counsellor at Law.

.. ..

We find within our breasts the active principles of humanity, social affection and generous sympathy. Out of this reflection springs a sweet reward for all the labours of benevolence.

BELISARIUS.

Juris præcepta sunt hæc : honeste vivere, alterum non lædere, suum cuique tribuere.

JUSTINIAN.

The poor shall never cease out of the land ; therefore I command thee, saying, thou shalt open thine hand *wide* unto thy brother, to thy poor, and to thy needy in thy land.

DEUT. xv. 11.

PRINTED by JOHN DENIO.
GREENFIELD—1810.

DISTRICT OF MASSACHUSETTS, *To wit* :

(L. S.) BE IT REMEMBERED, that on the 5th day of December, A. D. 1810, and in the thirty fifth year of the Independence of the United States of America, JONATHAN LEAVITT, of the said District, has deposited in this Office the Title of a Book, the right whereof he claims as Author, in the words following, *to wit* :

" A Summary of the Laws of Massachusetts, relative to the settlement, support, employment and removal of Paupers. By JONATHAN LEAVITT, Esq. *Counsellor at law.* We find within our breasts the active principles of humanity, social affection and generous sympathy. Out of this reflection springs a sweet reward for all the labors of benevolence.—BELISARIUS. Juris præcepta sunt hæc : honeste vivere, alterum non lædere, suum cuique tribuere. —JUSTINIAN. The poor shall never cease out of the land ; therefore I command thee, saying, thou shalt open thine hand *wide* unto thy brother, to thy poor, and to thy needy in thy land.— DEUT. XV. 11.

In conformity to the Act of the Congress of the United States, intitled, " An Act for the encouragement of learning, by securing the copies of maps, charts and books, to the authors and proprietors of such copies, during the times therein mentioned ;" and also to an Act intitled, " An Act supplementary to an Act, intitled, an Act for the encouragement of learning, by securing the copies of maps, charts and books, to the authors and proprietors of such copies during the times therein mentioned ; and extending the benefits thereof to the arts of designing, engraving and etching historical, and other Prints."

WM. S. SHAW,
Clerk of the District of Massachusetts.

INTRODUCTION.

THE ways and means of gaining legal settlements have been different in different periods of time. The time comprised in this Sketch is divided into five periods ; that is to say, between the year

1692	&	1701
1701		1767
1767		1789
1789		1794
1794		1810

During those periods, the law of settlement was different in one from what it was in the other. A full view of the law, as it existed in each period, would doubtless be a useful thing. A short view, if correct, may be of some service. That the one presented in the following pages may be, in some measure, serviceable, is the wish of the Author.

PERIOD I,

BETWEEN

1692 & 1701.

:::::::::::::::::::::::::::::::::::

IN this period there were five methods in which a settlement might be gained.

1. By marriage. A woman, by marrying, acquired the settlement of her husband, if he had any within the Commonwealth ; if not, she retained the one she had at the time of her marriage.

2. By parentage. Legitimate children had the settlement of their parents.

3. By birth. The birth place of illegitimate children was the place of their settlement. Bastards being considered as the children of nobody, and at the same time, as the children of the people, each town was holden to maintain such as happened to be born within its limits.

4. By slavery. While slavery was tolerated, the slave had the settlement of his master. And if the master died intestate, and administration was granted on his estate, the slave became the property of the administrator and acquired his settlement.—4 *Mass. Rep.* 123, & 539.

If a slave married a free man it is a question whether she gained a new derivative settlement by her marriage. So if a free woman married a slave it might well be questioned whether she gained a new settlement with a husband, who being the property of another had no claim to the service of the wife, and on whom the wife had no claim for maintenance. *Ibid.*

5. By a residence of three months, without warning. This method was provided by a statute of the late Province of Massachusetts, passed in the year 1692, and called the 4th of William and Mary.— By this statute it was enacted,

" That if any person or persons shall come to sojourn or dwell in any town within this Province or precinct thereof, and be there received and entertained for the space of three months, not having been warned by the Constable or other person whom the Selectmen shall appoint for that service, to leave the place, and the names of such persons, with the time of their abode there, and when such warning was given them, returned unto the Court of Quarter Sessions, every such person shall be reputed an inhabitant of such town, or precinct of the same ; and the proper charge of the same, in case through sickness, lameness, or otherwise they come to stand in need of relief, to be borne by such town ; unless the relations of such poor impotent person, in the line or degree of father or grand-father, mother or grand-mother, children or grand-children, be of sufficient ability ; then such relations respectively shall relieve such poor person, in such manner as the Justices of the Peace in that County where such sufficient persons dwell, shall assess, on pain that every one failing therein, shall forfeit *twenty shillings* for every month's neglect, to be levied by distress and sale of such offender's goods, by warrant from any two such Justices of the Peace *(Quorum Unus)* within their limits ; which shall be employed to the use and relief of such impotent poor person. *Provided nevertheless,* this Act shall not be understood of any persons committed to prison, or lawfully restrained in any town, or of such as shall come, or be sent for nursing or education, or to any physician or surgeon, to be healed or cured : but the particular persons who receive and entertain any such, shall be the town's security in their behalf ; and be obliged to relieve and support them in case of need ; upon complaint made to the Quarter Sessions, who shall accordingly order the same.

And any person orderly warned as aforesaid to depart any town whereof he is not an inhabitant, and neglecting so to do for the space of fourteen days next after such warning given, may by warrant from the next Justice of the Peace, be sent and conveyed from Constable to Constable, unto the town where he properly belongs, or had his last residence, at his own charge, if able to pay the same, or otherwise at the charge of the town so sending him."

In this method a settlement could be gained by such persons only as were competent to gain one in their own right. Such as were incompetent to this purpose, as married women, minors, slaves and persons lawfully restrained, gained no settlement by residence, in this, or in any other period. The settlements of such were derivative, and acquired by force of common law principles.

The *common law* of Massachusetts, in relation to settlements, is supposed to consit in the means and methods by which legal settlements have been acquired within the Commonwealth in ways not provided by any statute of the government.

A distinction is here made between *statute methods* and *common law methods*, of gaining a settlement.— *Statute methods* are defined to be the ways and means of gaining settlements provided by Acts of the Legislature. *Common law methods* are the means by which legal settlements have been acquired in ways not provided by any statute.

These definitions have reference only to the *general* statutes of the government. The legal effect of *special* Acts, by which unincorporated lands have been incorporated into towns, will be hereafter noticed.

A man competent to gain a settlement in his own right could not gain one by virtue of the common law, in this period, nor in any other. Such a man, if he gained a settlement at all, must have acquired it in a way provided by some Act of the Legislature.

The same may be said of women while sole and unmarried. A single woman, competent to gain a settlement in her own right, could not gain one by force of the common law, and still remain competent as aforesaid. She might, by marriage, cease to be competent in this respect, and at the same time acquire a new derivative settlement with her husband, in virtue of the common law.

As a residence of three months, without warning, was the only statute method of gaining a settlement that existed during this period, it follows that this was the only way in which a settlement could be gained by a person who was competent to gain one in his own right. He could not gain one by having and occupying a freehold estate, because no such way was provided by statute. And no such way existed at common law. It is true he could not be removed from his freehold as a pauper. But whenever he ceased to own and occupy a freehold estate, and become a pauper, he might then be removed, as such, to the place of his legal settlement.

PERIOD II.

:::::::::::::::::::::::::::::::::

IN this period there were seven ways of gaining a settlement.

1. By marriage.
2. By parentage.
3. By birth.
4. By slavery.
5. By twelve months residence, without warning.
6. By approbation of the town.
7. By approbation of the Selectmen.

The three methods last mentioned were provided by the following statute, paſſed in the year 1700 or 1701, and called the 12th and 13th of William 3d.

An Act directing the admission of town inhabitants.

" For the better preventing of persons obtruding themselves on any particular town within this Province, without orderly admission by the inhabitants of such town, or the Selectmen thereof, in maner as hereafter is expressed : And for remedying the manifold inconveniences and great charge heretofore occasioned thereby. To the intent also that the Selectmen may the more easily come to the certain knowledge of persons, and their circumstances that come to reside and sojourn in such town :

Be it enacted by the Lieutenant Governor, Council and Representatives in General Court assembled, and by the authority of the same, That every master of ship or other vessel arriving in any port within this Prov‑

B

ince, from any other country, land, island, colony
or plantation, at the time of entering his ship or
vessel with the receiver of impost, for the time being ; shall deliver to such receiver a perfect list or
certificate under his hand, of the christian and sir-
names of all passengers, as well servants as others,
brought in such ship or vessel, and their circumstances so far as he knows ; on pain of forfeiting
the sum of *five pounds*, to the use of the poor of the
town or place where such passengers shall be landed or sent on shore, for every passenger that he shall
omit to enter his or her name in such list or certificate ; upon conviction thereof before his majesty's
Justices in the court of General Sessions of the Peace,
within the same county where the offence is committed. And every Justice of the Peace is hereby
empowered, upon complaint made by the Selectmen
of such town, or some of them, to convent such
master before him, and to require and take sufficient security of him to appear and answer for his
said offence in manner as abovesaid ; such complainants also giving bond to prosecute their complaint.

And further it is enacted, That when it shall happen any passenger so brought, to be impotent, lame,
or otherwise infirm, or likely to be a charge to the
place ; if such person shall refuse to give security,
or cannot procure sufficient surety or sureties to become bound for his saving the town from such
charge ; in such case, the master of the ship or vessel in which such person came, shall be, and hereby
is obliged and required, to carry or send him or her
out of this Province again, within the space of two
months next after their arrival ; or otherwise to
give sufficient security as aforesaid, to indemnify
and keep the town free from all charge for the relief and support of such impotent, lame or infirm
person, upon demand thereof made by the Selectmen : unless such person was before an inhabitant

of this Province; or that such impotence, lameness, or other infirmity befel or happened to him or her during the passage : and in such case, if they be servants their masters shall provide for them, and others shall be relieved at the charge of the Province.

And the Justices of the General Sessions of the Peace, are hereby empowered to enjoin and order the performance of what is herein before required of such master accordingly.

And the receiver of impost is likewise required to inform and notify all masters of ships, and other vessels coming to him to enter, of the import of this act, and what is thereby enjoined and required of them : and not to admit an entry without such list or certificate, of the names of the passengers (if any) or that the master give under his hand that he brought none. And every such receiver shall forthwith transmit all lists or certificates of passengers, to the Town Clerk of such town where the ship or vessel that brought them shall lie, that the Selectmen may have knowlege of the same. And such Town Clerk is hereby required to lay all such lists or certificates returned to him, before the Selectmen at their next meeting.

And be it further enacted by the authority aforesaid, That from and after the publication of this act, no person whatsoever coming to reside or dwell within any town in this Province (other than freeholders or proprietors of land in such town, or those born, or that have served an apprenticeship there, and have not removed and become inhabitants elsewhere) shall be admitted to the privilege of elections in such town (though otherwise qualified) unless such person shall first make known his desire to the Selectmen thereof, and obtain their approbation, or the approbation of the town, for his dwelling there.

Nor shall any town be obliged to be at charge for the relief and support of any person residing in such town (in case he or she stand in need) that are not approved as aforesaid ; unless such person or persons have continued their residence there, for the space of twelve months next before, and have not been warned in manner as the Law directs, to depart and leave the town : any law, usage or custom to the contrary notwithstanding.

And if any person orderly warned to depart from any town whereof he or she is not an inhabitant, and being sent by warrant from a Justice of Peace unto the town whereto such person properly belongs, or to the place of his or her last abode, shall presume to return back, and obtrude him or herself upon the town so sent from, by residing there ; every person so offending, shall be proceeded against as a vagabond."

In 1736, an additional Act was made by which it was provided,

" That the inhabitants of the several towns, within this Province, who shall receive, admit and entertain any person or persons, not being inhabitants of such towns, either as inmates, boarders or tenants, in the house where such person dwells, or in any other house of his whatsoever, within this Province, or under any other qualifications, for more than the space of twenty days, and shall not, in writing, under their hands, give an account to one or more of the Selectmen, or the Town Clerk of such town, of all such person or persons so received, admitted or entertained by them, with the time they first received them, and the place from whence they last came, together with their circumstances, as far as they can ; shall, for every such neglect, forfeit and pay the sum of *forty shillings ;* to be recovered by bill, plaint or information, before any Justice of the Peace, or in any of his majesty's Courts of Record within this

Province ; the one half of the said fine to be employed to and for the use of the said poor of the
town where such offence shall be committ d ; the
other half to him or them that shall inform and sue
for the same : And they shall be liable to answer all
charges that may arise in the said town, by receiving and entertaining such person or persons as a-
foresaid ; to be recovered by the Town Treasurer ;
or Selectmen, where no Town Treasurer is appointed ; who are hereby respectively empowered to
bring an action accordingly.

SECT. 2. *And be it further enacted by the authority
aforesaid,* That all cost and charges, arising by
warning any such persons as are not inhabitants out
of town, entering the caution, or carrying them out
of town, shall be defrayed and paid by those who
received and entertained such person or persons in
their houses as aforesaid, and shall be recovered by
the Town Treasurer, or Selectmen, where no Treasurer is appointed ; who are hereby respectively empowered to bring an action accordingly.

And the Town Treasurer, or Selectmen of the
respective towns, in this Province, are hereby directed and ordered, before they bring their action,
to exhibit to such who receive and entertain any
person or persons in their houses as aforesaid, an
account of the charge arising thereby ; and upon
refusing to pay the same within five days, they shall
be liable to pay said charge, and be deprived of any
benefit by their notification, though given within
the twenty days as aforesaid."

In 1739, an explanatory statute was passed, by
which it was enacted, that,

" Notwithstanding the provision made by the act
passed in the twelfth and thirteenth years of King
William the third (intitled, an act directing the ad-

mission of town inhabitants) " That no town shall be obliged to be at charge for the support of any person residing there, unless such person have continued in such town (without being warned to depart thence) for the space of twelve months, or else have obtained the approbation of the town, or the Selectmen thereof, for his dwelling there :" Yet inasmuch as it is not expressly declared in what way and manner such approbation shall be given, some doubt hath thereupon arisen, whether the Selectmen or Assessors in any town, their rating or assessing any person residing there, to town charges, and the inhabitants reaping the benefit of his rate ought not (within the meaning of the said act) to have the force of an approbation for such person's dwelling there, so far as to subject such town to the charge of his support, in case he stands in need ; by means whereof sundry disputes, and expensive law suits have arisen and may arise, unless prevented by this court :

SECT. 1. *Be it therefore enacted by his excellency the Governor, Council and Representatives, in general court assembled, and by the authority of the same,* That no town shall be obliged to be at charge for the support of any person resident in such town that hath not continued there so long as to become an inhabitant, unless he have obtained the approbation of the town (at a meeting of the inhabitants regularly assembled) or the approbation of the Selectmen (at their meeting) for his dwelling there ; such approbation of the Selectmen to be given in writing, under their hands, or under the hands of the major part of them : And no act of the Selectmen or Assessors, in rating or assessing any such person unto any charges whatsoever, shall subject such town to any expenses for his support.

And whereas, upon the first paragraph in the act made in the fourth and fifth years of his present majesty's reign, and likewise that made in the tenth year of the same reign, directing the admission of town inhabitants, which relates to the charges which the inhabitants of any town shall be liable to answer, who shall admit and entertain any person (not being an inhabitant of such town) in his house as tenant or otherwise, for more than twenty days, and shall not, in writing, give such account to one of the Selectmen or Town Clerk of such town, as in said act is prescribed ; a doubt hath arisen whether the words [all charges] are to be construed to extend to the charges of supporting the persons so received and entertained, which may arise after he shall have continued in such town so long as to become an inhabitant :

SECT. 2. *Be it therefore declared and enacted by the authority aforesaid,* That the words [all charges] in the said paragraph do extend to, and include the charge of supporting the person so received and entertained after he shall have continued his residence in such town so long as to become an inhabitant ; and that such charges may be recovered at any time after they have arisen, although the term limited for the continuance of the said Act or Acts may (at the time of bringing the suit) be expired.

SECT. 3. *And it is hereby further declared and enacted by the authority aforesaid,* That no forbearance of the Selectmen to warn the person received and entertained as aforesaid to depart the town, shall free the inhabitant of such town by whom he was admitted and entertained, from the charge aforesaid, who shall violate the said Act by neglecting to give account or notice in manner as is therein directed. And each person offending (in violation of said Act) shall be liable to answer the whole of the charge incurred for the relief of the person by him admitted and entertained as aforesaid ; and all such charges are and ought to be understood and accounted to have arisen and accrued to the town by reason only of such his misdeed and neglect ; any others in like manner offending notwithstanding.

And that the several Acts aforesaid, are and were intended as herein explained, and ought always so to be understood and put in execution."

The aforesaid statute of William 3d. gave the privilege of elections to freeholders, proprietors of land, persons born in a town, and such as had served an apprenticeship there, and had not become inhabitants elsewhere. But no settlement was gained by being entitled to this privilege. A person entitled to it could not acquire a settlement by virtue of this Act, in any way except in one of the three methods last mentioned.

The requisites of a legal warning were the same in this period as in the first. They are particularly pointed out in that part of the statute of William and Mary which is recited in the first period.

If a man was legally warned to depart from a town, and thereby prevented from gaining a settlement himself, the consequence was that his wife, child and slave were also prevented, though not named in the warning, because they were incapable of gaining a settlement in their own right.——3 *Mass. Rep.* 322.

If a person was duly warned to depart from a town, and after the warning removed therefrom, without an intention of returning, continuing absent long enough to gain a new settlement, and afterwards came back and dwelt in the same town, he must have been again warned within one year from the time of his return, or he would have gained a settlement.——4 *Mass. Rep.* 131.

If a mariner made it his home in a town for one year without warning, and followed the business of his profession therefrom, he thereby gained a settlement.——4 *Mass. Rep.* 312.

PERIOD III.

BETWEEN

1767 & 1789.

::::::::::::::::::::::::::::::::::

IN this period there were four methods in which a settlement might be gained.

1. By marriage.
2. By parentage.
3. By slavery,
4. By approbation of the town.

The method last mentioned was provided by a statute of the 7th Geo. 3, which was published on the 20th of March, 1767, and is sometimes called the statue of '67—and is as follows:

An Act in addition to the several laws already made relating to the removal of poor persons out of the towns whereof they are not inhabitants.

" Whereas in and by an act passed in the fourth year of the reign of their late majesties King William and Queen Mary, intitled an Act for regulating of townships, choice of town officers, and setting forth their power ; it is among other things enacted, " That any person orderly warned to depart any town whereof he is not an inhabitant, and neglecting so to do for the space of fourteen days next after such warning given, may by warrant of the next Justice of the Peace be sent and conveyed from Constable to Constable, unto the town where he properly belongs, or had his last residence, at his own charge if able to pay the same, or otherwise at the charge of the town so sending him."

C

And whereas it frequently happens that the persons so sent, and conveyed by warrant as aforesaid, do not properly belong to, nor had their last lawful residence in any town in this Province, but are inhabitants of some other Province or Colony, and are poor and unable to pay the charge of such their removal, whereby an unequal charge and burthen arises to the towns to which such poor persons happen to come.

For remedy whereof, and to the end that such charges may be borne in a more equitable and just proportion,

Be it enacted by the Governor, Council, and House of Representatives, That when and so often as any such person or persons are to be sent or conveyed out of this Province, it shall and may be lawful for any Justice of the Peace of the county from whence the person or persons are to be sent or conveyed, and he is hereby empowered to grant a warrant for sending such person or persons out of the Province, either by land or water, as he shall think will be most convenient, or least liable to charge.

And be it further enacted, That when and so often as it shall happen that any person so to be sent and conveyed, either by land or water, as shall be thought most convenient, by warrant as aforesaid, doth not properly belong to, nor had gained a fettlement in any town in this Province, but is an inhabitant of, or had a settlement in some one of his majesty's Provinces or Colonies on this Continent ; then and in every such case the charge of conveying such person or persons, shall be borne by said person or persons, if able to pay the same ; otherwise to be borne and paid by this Province, in order to their being sent or conveyed to the Province or Colony where they last had a settlement ; and the Constable or Constables of each town respectively to whom such warrant shall be directed, to convey such person or persons by land ; and to whose care such per-son or persons shall be committed, shall by virtue of said warrant, receive and convey him, her or them through the county to which he belongs, and to one of the Conftables of the next town in the next county, who shall by virtue of said warrant re-ceive the said person or persons, and convey him, her or them through the county in which such Con-stable dwells ; and the said person or persons, shall by virtue of the warrant aforesaid, be conveyed by the Constable from county to county in the same manner, unto the Province or Colony to which he, she or they shall be first ordered ; and every Con-stable so receiving and conveying such person or persons shall receive out of the Treasury of such town where he belongs, so much money as the Se-lectmen of such town shall think the charge of con-veying such person or persons as aforesaid, through the county shall amount to ; the said Constable to keep a fair account of his trouble and expense, and exhibit the same to the said Selectmen, who are to consider and adjust the same ; and the said Select-men are also hereby empowered and directed to adjust and pay the charge of conveying any person or per-sons by water as aforesaid ; they to receive the same again out of the Province Treasury.

And be it further enacted, That when and so often as any person or persons to be removed, shall be an inhabitant or inhabitants, of any town or district within this Province, they shall be conveyed to such town or district where he, she or they are inhabit-ants, or have a settlement, in the same manner as is herein before provided in cases where the persons so removed are not inhabitants of any town within this Province, the charge of such conveyance to be paid as by a law of this Province is already provided.

And be it further enacted, That from and after the tenth day of April next, no person whatsoever coming to reside or dwell within any town in this Province, shall gain an inhabitancy in such town by any length of time he or she may continue there without warning, unless such person shall first have made known his or her desire to the Selectmen thereof, and obtained the approbation of the town, at a general meeting of the inhabitants for his dwelling there ; nor shall any town be obliged to be at charge for the relief and support of any person residing in such town (in case he or she stand in need) that have not been approved as aforesaid : And all such persons as have not been approved as aforesaid, together with their children, whether born before or after their coming to such town, in wedlock, or otherwise, shall be liable to be sent or conveyed to the town where they properly belong, by a warrant from a Justice of the Peace, who is hereby empowered upon application from the Selectmen of the town from which such person or persons are to be sent to issue his warrant acccordingly, excepting for such as are apprentices to some inhabitant or inhabitants of such town, who shall not be liable to be sent or conveyed out of any town where they are apprentices, till the time of their apprenticeship is expired, any law, usage, or custom to the contrary notwithstanding.

And be it further enacted, That every Constable shall before he delivers said warrant to the Constable of the next county certify his doings thereon.

This act to continue and be in force for the space of three years, and no longer."

This was a temporary act, and is said to have expired, for a short time, but was soon revived and continued in force until the 23d of June, 1789.

By the operation of this statute the common law method of gaining a settlement by *birth* was abrogated. In the case of Chelsea against Malden, 4

Mass. Rep. 135, the court say that "by this statute no settlement could be gained by *birth.*" Consequently, in this period illegitimate children acquired their settlement by parentage ; the place of their mother's settlement being the place of their settlement.

The method of gaining a settlement by slavery continued in force until the year 1780, when it was abolished by the adoption of the present conftitution of the Commonwealth.

A question has been made, under this statute, whether a person, by purchasing a freehold estate, and living upon it, did thereby gain a settlement in the town where it lay. And, in the case of Salem against Andover, the court were strongly inclined to think he did not. They said " It is a reasonable construction that by force of this statute a man shall not be removed from his freehold. But he may not gain a settlement by purchasing and living on his own freehold. For immovability does not necessarily imply a settlement. So the statute of 1793, c. 34 (passed the 11th of February, 1794) enacts that any person having a freehold estate of ten dollars per annum in the place where he dwells, and taking the rents and profits thereof three years successively, shall gain a settlement. But a freehold of less annual value will not give a settlement, although the owner may not be removeable from it against his consent. But we do not think it necessary now to decide this point."—*3 Mass. Rep.* 436.

Afterwards in the case of Bath against Bowdoin, in error, it seems to have been considered that having a freehold estate in a town in the year 1774, and living upon it, did not, at that time, give a settlement.—*4 Mass. Rep.* 452.

The conclusion is that, during this period, a settlement could not be gained by having and occupying a freehold estate. And for the same reason it is concluded that a settlement could not be gained by having and occupying such estate in the second period : because the aforesaid acts of 1701 & 1767 were substantially the same so far as either of them could have any effect upon this question ; and because the reason suggested why a settlement could not be gained, in the first period, by having and occupying a freehold estate, applies with equal force against the supposition that a settlement could be gained, either in the second or third period, by owning and occupying such estate.

Every legal settlement gained within the Commonwealth, either in the first, second or third period, must have been acquired by virtue of the common law, or by force of some statute of the government. But no statute existed, in either of those periods, which provided that a settlement might be gained by having and occupying a freehold estate, and no such way existed by virtue of the common law. Consequently a settlement could not be gained in either of those periods by having and occupying such estate.

PERIOD IV.

BETWEEN

1789 & 1794,

::::::::::::::::::::::::::::::::::::::

ON the 23d of June, 1789, the following statute was enacted.

An act determining what transactions shall be necessary to constitute the settlement of a citizen in any particular Town or District.

1. " *Be it enacted by the Senate and House of Representatives in General Court assembled, and by the authority of the same,* That all persons, citizens of this Commonwealth, who, before the tenth day of April, one thousand seven hundred and sixty seven, resided or dwelt within any town or district in the then Province of the Massachusetts Bay, for the space of one year, not having been warned to depart therefrom according to law, or who since the same tenth day of April, have obtained the approbation of the town or district, at a general meeting of the inhabitants, for his dwelling there, or who have obtained a legal settlement in such town or district, by birth, marriage, or otherwise, and have not afterwards gained a settlement elsewhere, in this, or some other of the United States, shall be deemed and taken to be inhabitants of the same town or district, to every intent and purpose whatever. And every person being a citizen of this Commonwealth, who shall be seized of an estate of freehold, in any particular town or district, of the clear annual income of *three pounds,* and shall reside thereon, or within the same town or district, occupying and improving the same

in person, for the space of two whole years, or who, after the age of twenty one years, shall reside and pay a town tax, for the term of five years successively, or shall reside in such town or district for the space of two years successively, without being warned to depart the same in manner hereafter provided, shall be deemed and taken to be an inhabitant of the same town or district.

2. *And be it further enacted by the authority aforesaid,* That any citizen of this Commonwealth, who shall have and obtain the vote of any town or district at a regular meeting, to be admitted and received an inhabitant thereof, shall, from and after the passing such vote, in case such citizen shall there reside and dwell, be deemed and taken to be an inhabitant of the same.

3. *And be it further enacted by the authority aforesaid,* That every woman, by intermarrying with an inhabitant of any town or district, shall by such marriage be deemed and taken to be an inhabitant of the same town or district with her husband ; and children born in wedlock, at the time of their birth and afterwards, shall be deemed and taken as inhabitants of the same town or district with their parents; and children otherwise born, shall be deemed and taken to be inhabitants with the mother, until they shall have obtained a legal settlement or habitancy in some other town or district ; but no person shall have more than one place of legal settlement at one and the same time, but upon obtaining a new place of settlement, shall be deemed and taken voluntarily to have relinquished any former one.

4. *Provided always,* That no person committed to prison, or lawfully detained in any town or district, or who shall come or be sent for nursing, education or support, or to learn any trade or mystery, or who shall come or be sent to any Physician or Surgeon, to be cured of any disorder, shall, by remain-

ing in such town or district for any length of time, in consequence thereof, obtain a settlement therein.

5. *Be it further enacted by the authority aforesaid,* That when any person shall come into any town or district within this Commonwealth to reside, not entitled to habitancy by the qualifications before recited in this act, the Selectmen of such town or district shall be, and they are hereby empowered to warn such person to depart the limits of such town or district.

6. *And be it further enacted by the authority aforesaid,* That the method of warning a person to depart from any town or district, shall be in writing under the hands and seals of the Selectmen, or the major part of them, in substance as follows, viz.

(Seal.)————ss.

To either of the Constables of the Town of in *said County,* Greeting.

You are, in the name of the Commonwealth of Massachusetts, directed to warn and give notice unto A. B. of in the county of labourer, (or a transient person, as the case may be) who has lately come into this town for the purpose of abiding therein, not having obtained the town's consent therefor, that he (or she) depart the limits thereof (with their children, and others under their care, if such they have) within fifteen days. And of this precept, with your doings thereon, you are to make return into the office of the Clerk of the town or district within twenty days next coming, that such further proceedings may be had in the premises as the law directs. Given under our hands and seals at aforesaid, this day of A. D. Selectmen of

And the mode of service shall be by reading or delivering a copy of the precept to the person ordered to depart, or by leaving a copy of such precept at his or her last and usual place of abode; and it

D

shall be the duty of the town or district Clerk, to make a record of the warrant, and the return of the Constable made thereon, in the town book.

7. *And be it further enacted by the authority aforesaid,* That all former laws for fixing or determining the habitancy or settlement of citizens, touching settlements hereafter to be obtained, be and hereby are repealed."

This statute provided six methods by which a settlement might be acquired.

1. By having a freehold estate of the annual income of 10 dollars, and residing thereon, or within the same town, occupying and improving the same in person for the space of two whole years.

This method took effect although the occupant was warned to depart within the two years.—3 *Mass. Rep.* 436, & 4 *Mass. Rep.* 495.

A man seized of a freehold estate in right of another, as in right of his wife, and occupying the same two years thereby gained a settlement. A wife, however could not have a freehold in the land of her deceased husband, in this, or in any other period, until an assignment of her dower was made by the heir, or other tenant, or by legal proceedings.—4 *Mass. Rep.* 384.

A freehold is an estate in fee, or for life. Estates for years, at will, or by sufferance, are not freeholds. An estate for a thousand years is not a freehold.— *Co. Lit.* 6.

2. By residing in and paying a town tax for the term of five years successively.

This method never went into operation: because it was less than five years from the passing of this act to the time of its repeal; which took place on the 11th of February, 1794.

3. By a residence of two years, without warning. This method never took effect. The term of res-

idence prescribed by this statute was extended to three years by an act passed the 9th of March, 1791 : and by an act passed the 6th of March, 1792, was prolonged to four years : and afterwards was further extended to five years by an act passed the 22d of March, 1793. And before the five years elapsed all these acts were repealed. So that since the 10th of April, 1767, there has been no time when a settlement could be gained by residence merely.

4. By vote of the town.

5. By marriage. ⎫ These common law methods
6. By parentage. ⎭ of gaining a settlement were incorporated into the act just recited, and thereby were changed into statute methods. So that in this period, it is supposed, there were no common law methods in which a settlement could be gained.

PERIOD V,

BETWEEN
1794 & 1810.

:::::::::::::::::::::::::::::::::::

ON the 11th of February, 1794, the following law was passed.

An Act ascertaining what shall constitute a legal settlement of any person, in any Town or District within the Commonwealth, so as to entitle him to support therein, in case he becomes poor and stands in need of relief ; and for repealing all Laws heretofore made respecting such settlement.

" 1. *Be it enacted by the Senate and House of Representatives in General Court assembled, and by the authority of the same,* That all Laws heretofore made, enacting and ascertaining what shall consitute

Laws repealed.

a legal settlement of any person in any town or district withint his Commonwealth, so as to subject and oblige such town or district to support such person in case of his becoming poor and standing in need of relief, so far as they relate to the manner of gaining a settlement in future, be, and they hereby are repealed ; but all settlements al-

Settlements to remain.

ready gained by force of said laws, or otherwise, shall remain, until lost by gaining others in some of the ways hereafter mentioned.

2. *And be it further enacted,* That legal settlements in any town or district in this Common-

Ways & means providing legal settlements in case of poverty.

wealth, shall be hereafter gained so as to subject and oblige such town or district to relieve and support the persons gaining the same, in case they become poor and stand in need of relief, by the ways and means following, and not otherwise, namely :

First. A married woman shall always fol- Married
low and have the settlement of her husband, women.
if he have any within this Commonwealth, otherwise her own at the time of marriage, if she then
had any, shall not be lost or suspended by the marriage ; and in case the wife shall be removed to her
settlement, and the husband shall want relief from
the State, he shall receive it in the town where his
wife shall have her settlement, at the expense of the
Commonwealth.

Second. Legitimate children shall follow Legitimate
and have the settlement of their father, if children.
he shall have any within this Commonwealth, until
they gain a settlement of their own ; but if he shall
have none, they shall, in like manner, follow and
have the settlement, of their mother, if she shall
have any.

Third. Illegitimate children shall follow Illegitimate.
and have the settlement of their mother, at the time
of birth, if any she shall then have within the Commonwealth ; but neither legitimate nor illegitimate
children shall gain a settlement by birth in the places
where they may be born, if neither of their parents
shall then have any settlement there.

Fourth. Any person of twenty one years Other des-
of age, being a citizen of this or any of the criptions of
United States, having an estate of inherit- persons.
ance or freehold in the town or district where he
dwells and has his home, of the clear yearly income
of *three pounds,* and taking the rents & profits thereof
three years successively, whether he lives thereupon
or not, shall thereby gain a settlement therein.

Fifth. Any person of twenty one years of age, being a citizen of this or any of the United States,
having an estate, the principal of which shall be set
at *sixty pounds,* or the income of *three pounds twelve
shillings,* in the valuation of estates made by the Assessors, and being assessed for the same, to state,

county, town or district taxes, for the space of five years successively, in the town or district where he dwells, and has his home, shall thereby gain a settlement therein.

Sixth. Any person being chosen and actually serving one whole year, in the office of Clerk, Treasurer, Selectman, Overseer of the poor, Assessor, Constable, or Collector of taxes in any town or district, shall thereby gain a settlement therein.

Seventh. All settled ordained Ministers of the Gospel shall be deemed as legally settled in the towns or districts wherein they are or may be settled and ordained.

Eighth. Any person that shall be admitted an inhabitant by any town or district at any legal meeting, in the warrant, for which an article shall be inserted for that purpose, shall thereby gain a legal settlement therein.

Ninth. All persons, citizens as aforesaid, dwelling and having their homes in any unincorporated place, at the time when the same shall be incorporated into a town or district, shall thereby gain a legal settlement therein.

Tenth. Upon a division of towns or districts, every person having a legal settlement therein, but being removed therefrom at the time of such division, and not having gained a legal settlement elsewhere, shall have his legal settlement in that town or district wherein his former dwelling place or home shall happen to fall upon such division ; and when any new town or district shall be incorporated, composed of a part of one or more old incorporated towns or districts, all persons legally settled in the town or towns, district or districts, of which such new town or district is so composed, and who shall actually dwell and have their homes within the bounds of such new town or district at the time of its incorporation, shall thereby gain legal settlement in such new town or district.

Provided nevertheless, That no person re- Proviso. siding in that part of any town or district, which upon such division shall be incorporated into a new town or district, having then no legal settlement therein, shall gain any by force of such incorporation only ; nor shall such incorporation prevent his gaining a settlement therein within the time and by the means by which he would have gained it there, if no such division had been made.

Eleventh. Any minor who shall serve an apprenticeship to any lawful trade for the space of four years, in any town or district, and actually set up the same therein, within one year after the expiration of said term, being then twenty one years old, and continue to carry on the same for the space of five years therein, shall thereby gain a settlement in such town or district ; but such person, being hired as a journeyman, shall not be considered as setting up a trade.

Twelfth. Any person, being a citizen, as aforesaid, and of the age of twenty one years, who shall hereafter reside in any town or district within this Commonwealth for the space of ten years together, and pay all state, county, town or district taxes, duly assessed on such person's poll or estate, for any five years within said time, shall thereby gain a settlement in such town or district.

And every legal settlement when gained shall continue till lost or defeated by gaining a new one ; and upon gaining such new settlement all former settlements shall be defeated and lost."

By this statute, which is now in force, there are eleven ways in which a settlement may be gained.

1. By marriage.
2. By parentage. Legitimate children follow and have the settlement of their father, if he has any within the Commonwealth, until they gain one of

their own ; but if he has none, they follow and
have the settlement of their mother, if she has any.

It has been contended that all legitimate children,
by virtue of this provision of law, *of whatever age
they may be*, follow and have the settlement of their
father until they gain one for themselves. But in
the case of Springfield against Wilbraham the Court
say, " In the construction of this clause of the statute we are all of opinion that upon the father's
gaining a new settlement, a child of full age, although voluntarily living with him, does not have
the new settlement of his father, but his former settlement remains. Whether the case of a child being non compos, or of a son marrying under age,
or enlisting as a soldier, by which, during the en-
listment, the father has lost all controul over his
person, or right to the profits of his services, are
or are not exceptions, may be determined when
those cases arise. The present is not one of them.

We find cases in the English reports where a child
of full age, living with his father, is considered as
not emancipated. In those cases the child may be
considered as a servant ; and in that country a settlement may be acquired by service. But by our
laws no settlement can be acquired by service."—4.
Mass. Rep. 493.

Illegitimate children follow and have the settlement of their mother. This has been the case ever
since the 10th of April 1767. Before that time the
place of their birth was the place of their settlement.

3. By having an estate of inheritance or freehold,
of the annual income of 10 dollars, and taking the
profits thereof three years successively.

A freehold of less yearly income gives no settlement. Yet the owner may not be removed from it
against his consent.—3 *Mass. Rep.* 436.

An inheritance is an estate in land, or in some-
thing appurtenant thereto, holden by one to himself

and his heirs. A grant to one, his heirs and assigns, of all the trees and timber standing and growing in a close forever, with free liberty to cut and carry them away at pleasure, conveys an *estate of inheritance* in the trees and timber.——4 *Mass. Rep.* 266.—— Every estate of inheritance is a freehold ; but every freehold is not an estate of inheritance.

4. By being chosen and actually serving one year in certain town offices mentioned in the statute.

But no settlement is gained by being chosen and serving as representative, or in any other office not mentioned in the act.

5. By having an estate at 200 dollars, or an income of 12 dollars, and being assessed for the same five years successively, as pointed out in the statute.

6. By becoming a settled ordained minister of the gospel.

7. By vote of the town.

8. By dwelling in an unincorporated place at the time when it is incorporated.

This method of gaining a settlement now takes effect by force of the *general* statute last recited. In former periods, the legal effect of *special* acts of incorporation was substantially the same.——" If the territory of which a new town was composed, had before been an unincorporated place, the incorporation would *ipso facto* have given every one inhabiting there a legal settlement."——4 *Mass. Rep.* 452.

9. By the division of a town or district.

When a town is divided the effect of such division may be considered with reference to three descriptions of persons.

First. Persons then dwelling in the town and having a legal settlement there. Such retain their settlement in the old town, unless, upon the division, their dwelling place happens to fall within the limits of the new town. If that happens, then they lose their settlement in the old town, and acquire one in the new town.——4 *Mass. Rep.* 417.

Second. Persons dwelling in the town when it is divided but having no legal settlement there. Such gain no settlement in consequence of the division, although their dwelling place happens, on the division, to fall within the limits of the new town. Nor are they prevented from gaining one in the same time, way and manner they would have done, if the division had not have taken place.——4 *Mass. Rep.* 487.

Third. Persons having a legal settlement in the town when it is divided, but being, at that time, removed out of it, and absent from it. Such have their settlement in that town wherein their former dwelling place, from which they removed, happens to fall upon such division. This has been the case since the passing of the act last recited. Before that time, such absent persons retained their settlement in the old town, although their former dwelling place, from which they removed, happened, on the division, to fall within the limits of the new town.—4 *Mass. Rep.* 280, 348, & 679.

10. By serving an apprenticeship, setting up the trade, and carrying it on, as specified in the statute.

11. By a residence of ten years, and payment of all taxes for any five years within that time.

A settlement once gained in any town in the state is not lost but by gaining another in some place within the state.——4 *Mass. Rep.* 133.

On the 26th of February, 1794, the following act was passed.

An act providing for the relief and support, employment and removal of the poor, and for repealing all former laws made for those purposes.

" 1. *BE it enacted by the Senate and House of Representatives in General Court assembled, and by the authority of the same,* That every town and district within this Commonwealth shall be holden to relieve and support all poor and indigent persons, lawfully settled therein, whenever they shall stand in need thereof; and may vote and raise monies therefor, and for their employment, in the same way that monies for other town or district charges are voted and raised : And may, also, at their annual meeting, choose any number, not exceeding twelve, of suitable persons, dwelling therein, to be Overseers of their Poor, and where such are not specially chosen, the Selectmen shall be Overseers of the Poor, *ex officio.*

Towns authorised to support poor.

—to choose Overseers.

2. *Be it further enacted,* That said Overseers shall have the care and oversight of all such poor and indigent persons, so settled in their respective towns and districts ; and shall see that they are suitably relieved, supported and employed, either in the work house or other tenements belonging to such towns or districts, or in such other way and manner, as they, at any legal meeting, shall direct, or otherwise at the discretion of said Overseers, at the cost of such town or district.

—who shall have the care thereof.

3. *Provided always, and be it further enacted,* That the kindred of any such poor person, if any he shall have, in the line or degree of father or grandfather, mother or grandmother, children or grandchildren, by consanguinity, living within this Commonwealth, of sufficient ability, shall be holden to support such pauper, in proportion to such ability.

Proviso.

And the Court of Common Pleas in the County where any of such kindred to be charged shall reside,

Court of Common Pleas authorised, in case of supporting poor.

upon complaint made by any town or district, or kindred who shall have been at any expense for the relief and support of any such pauper (which complaint being filed in the Clerk's office of such Court, and summons thereon issued, directed to and served by any proper Officer to serve original summons, and in the manner they are by law to be served, fourteen days before the sitting of such Court, shall be sufficient to hold the persons summoned to answer thereto) may on due hearing, either upon the appearance or default of the kindred so summoned, assess and apportion such sum as they shall judge reasonable therefor, upon such of said kindred as they shall judge of sufficient ability, and according thereto, to the time of such assessment, with costs, and may enforce payment thereof

Proviso.

by warrant of distress : *Provided* such assessment shall not extend to any expense for any relief afforded more than six months previous to the filing of such complaint.

And may further assess and apportion upon them, such weekly sum for the future, as they shall judge sufficient for the support of such pauper, to be paid quarterly till further order of Court, and upon application from time to time of the town, district or kindred, to whom the same shall have been ordered to be paid, the Clerk of said Court shall issue, and may renew a warrant of distress for the arrears of any preceding quarter.

And the Court may further order, with whom of such kindred, that may desire it, such pauper shall live and be relieved, and for such time with one, and such with another, as they shall judge proper, having regard to the comfort of the pauper, as well as the convenience of the kindred. And upon suggestion, other kindred of ability, not named in the complaint, may be notified, and the process may be continued, and upon due notice, whether they appear or are defaulted, the Court may proceed against them in the same manner as if they had been named in the complaint. But if such complaint be not entered, or be discontinued or withdrawn, or be adjudged groundless, the respondents shall recover costs.

And such Court may take further order from time to time in the premises, upon application of any party interested, and may alter such assessment and apportionment as the circumstances may vary.

4. *And be it further enacted,* That said Overseers be, and they hereby are empowered, from time to time, to bind out, by deed indented or poll, as apprentices, to be instructed and employed in any lawful art, trade or mystery, or as servants to be employed in any lawful work or labor, any male or female children, whose parents are lawfully settled in, and become actually chargeable to their town or district ; also, whose parents, so settled, shall be thought by said Overseers to be unable to maintain them, (whether they receive alms, or are so chargeable or not) *Provided,* they be not assessed to any town or district charges ; and also all such who, or whose parents residing in their town or district, are supported there at the charge of the Commonwealth, or whose parents are unable to support them as aforesaid, to any citizen of this Commonwealth—that is to say, male children till they come to the age of twenty one years, and females till they come to the age of eighteen, or are married ; which binding shall be valid and effectual in law, as if such children had been of the full age of twenty one years, and had by a like deed bound themselves, or their parents had

(margin notes: Overseers authorised to bind out poor children. Proviso.)

been consenting thereto ; Provision to be made in such deed for the instruction of male children so bound out, to read, write and cypher, and of females to read and write, and for such other instruction, benefit and allowance, either within or at the end of the term, as to the Overseers may seem fit and reasonable.

5. *And be it further enacted,* That it shall be the duty of said Overseers, to inquire into the usage of children already legally bound out, or that may be bound out by force of this act, and to defend them from injuries. And upon complaint, by such Overseers made to the Court of Common Pleas, in the county where their town or district is, or where the child may be bound, against the master of any such child, for abuse, ill treatment or neglect ; said Court (having duly notified the party complained of) may proceed to hear the complaint, and if the same be supported, and the cause shall be judged sufficient, may liberate and discharge such child from his or her master, with costs, for which execution may be awarded, otherwise the complaint shall be dismissed, but without costs, unless it appear groundless and without probable cause, in which case costs shall be allowed the respondent.

Duty of Overseers respecting such children.

Court of Common Pleas authorised in case.

Any apprentice or servant so discharged, or whose master shall decease, may be bound out anew, for the remainder of the term, in manner aforesaid. And such Overseers may also have remedy by action on such deed, against any person liable thereby, for recovery of damages for breaches of any of the covenants therein contained, which when recovered, shall be placed in the town or district treasury, deducting reasonable charges,

Apprentices discharged may be bound anew.

and disposed of by the Overseers at their discretion ; for the benefit and relief of such apprentice or servant within the term ; the remainder, if any, to be paid him at the expiration thereof ; and the Court before which such cause shall be tried originally, and on the appeal, may also, upon the plaintiff's request, if they see cause, liberate and discharge such apprentice or servant from his master, if it hath not been already done in the method before directed by this act. And such apprentice or servant shall have like remedy when their term is expired, for damages for the causes aforesaid, other than such (if any) for which damages may have been recovered as aforesaid, by action upon such deed to be delivered them for that purpose, and on which no endorsement shall be necessary : *Provided*, such action be commenced within two years after the expiration of the term ; and where such deed shall have before been put in suit, an attested copy from the proper Officer may be used and have the same force as the original. And no action brought by Overseers shall abate by the death of some of them, or by their being succeeded in office, pending the action, but it shall proceed in the names of the original plaintiffs or the survivors of them.

Power of Overseers.

Proviso.

And in case of elopements, any such apprentice or servant may be apprehended by any Justice of the Peace, of the county where he is bound or where he may be found, upon complaint of the master, or any other on his behalf, and returned to his master by any person to whom the warrant may be directed, or may be first sent to the house of correction, at the Justice's direction. And every person enticing any such apprentice or servant to elope from his master, or harbouring him, knowing him to have eloped,

In case of elopement.

Persons enticing to elope liable.

shall be liable to the master's action for all damages sustained thereby. And the Court of Common Pleas, either in the county where the Overseers binding, or the master of any apprentice or servant bound, live, may also upon complaint of such master, for gross misbehaviour, discharge such apprentice or servant from his apprenticeship or service, after due notice to such Overseers, and hearing thereupon.

6. *And be it further enacted,* That said Overseers shall have power to set to work, or bind out to service by deed as aforesaid, for a term not exceeding one whole year at a time, all such persons, residing and lawfully settled in their respective towns or districts, or who have no such settlement within this Commonwealth, married or unmarried, upwards of twenty one years of age, as are able of body, but have no visible means of support, who live idly, and use and exercise no ordinary or daily lawful trade or business to get their living by ; and also all persons who are liable by any law to be sent to the house of correction, upon such terms and conditions as they shall think proper.

Overseers authorised respecting persons of age.

7. *Provided always,* That any person thinking him or herself aggrieved by the doings of said Overseers, in the premises, may apply by complaint to the Court of Common Pleas, in the county where they are bound or where the Overseers who bound them dwell, for relief ; which Court, after due notice to the Overseers, and to their masters, shall have power, after due hearing and examination, if they find sufficient cause, to liberate and discharge the party complaining from his or her master, and to release him or her from the care of the Overseers, otherwise to dismiss the complaint, and to give costs to either party or not, as the Court may think reasonable.

Proviso.

8. *And be it further enacted*, That the poor persons standing in need of relief living without the bounds of any incorporated town or district, shall be under the care of the Overseers of the poor, appointed in the adjoining town or district, wherein the inhabitants of such unincorporated place are usually

Authorised respecting those poor who live without the bounds of incorporated towns.

taxed : And the same Overseers shall have the like authority to bind out the children of such poor persons, as they are vested with, respecting the children of persons in like circumstances, inhabitants of the town or district in which they are appointed. And such Overseers may also set to work, or bind out as aforesaid, for a space not exceeding one whole year at a time, all such persons above the age of twenty one years, married or unmarried, residing in their county, but without the bounds of any town or district, as are able of body, but have no visible means of support, or who live idly, using no ordinary, daily lawful trade or business to get their living by, or who are liable by any law, to be sent to the house of correction, and shall receive and apply their earnings, (deducting reasonable charges) to the support of them or their families, if any they have, at their discretion, saving to such persons the like remedy for relief, if they think themselves aggrieved, as is by this act provided for persons set to work, or bound out for like causes by Overseers of towns.

And for the prevention of poverty as well as lewdness,

9. *Be it further enacted*, That any person who shall be suspected of keeping a house of ill fame, resorted to for the purpose of prostitution or lewdness, may be apprehended by warrant from any Justice of the Peace in the county, upon complaint of the Overseers of the town or district wherein such house shall be ; and upon

house of ill fame to be broke up.

F

conviction of such offence before such Justice, or before the Court of General Sessions of the Peace, or presentment of the Grand Jury, may be ordered to the house of correction, for a term not exceeding one month ; and after such conviction, shall not be allowed to keep lodgers or boarders, in any town or district, without the license of the Overseers of the poor thereof.

10. *And be it further enacted,* That it shall also be the duty of said Overseers, in their respective towns or districts, to provide for the immediate comfort and relief of all persons residing, or found therein, not belonging thereto, but having lawful settlements in other towns or districts, when they fall into distress, and stand in need of immediate relief, and until they shall be removed to the places of their lawful settlements, the expenses whereof, incurred within three months next before notice given to the town or district, to be charged, as also of their removal, or of their burial, in case of their decease, may be sued for and recovered, either in a civil action, by the town or district incurring the same, against the town or district wherein such persons had such settlements, or in the method by complaint, hereafter prescribed in and by this act ; *provided,* such action or complaint for damages be commenced or preferred within two years after the cause of action arose, but not otherwise. And in such civil action, the settlement of the pauper shall not be contested by the defendants, if it hath been then adjudged to be in their town or district upon such process as is herein after prescribed ; otherwise it may be : And a recovery in such action shall bar the town or district, against which the same shall be had, from disputing the settlement of such pauper, in such town

Overseers authorised to provide for strangers.

at the expense of their own town.

Proviso

or district, with the town or district so recovering, in any future action or process, brought and prosecuted for the support or removal of such pauper.

11. *And be it further enacted,* That all persons actually chargeable, or who, through age or infirmity, idleness or dissoluteness, are likely to become chargeable to the places wherein they are found, but in which they have no lawful settlements, may be removed to the places of their lawful settlements, if they have any within the Commonwealth. And in order to effect such removal, (and also to recover the expences incurred for the relief of such persons, if said Overseers choose that mode in preference to a civil action) said Overseers may apply by complaint, to any Justice of the Peace in their county, not an inhabitant of their town or district, which complaint may be in substance, as follows :

Paupers to be removed to their lawful settlements

TO　　　a Justice of the Peace, in and for the county of　　　The town of　　　in the said county, by the subscribers, Overseers of their poor, complain and shew, that　　　now resident in said town, is poor, and become chargeable to said town ; and that his lawful settlement is in　　　in the county of Wherefore your complainants pray that after a due course of proceedings had, the lawful settlement of said　　　may be adjudged to be in said town of　　　, and that he may be removed thither by warrant accordingly. Your complainants further pray judgment for damages, for expences incurred on account of said　　　an account whereof is annexed, and for such as may accrue until the time of judgment, and for costs. Dated at said　　　the day of　　　A. D. 17　.

form of complaint.

A. B. &c. Overseers.

Upon which complaint, such Justice shall make out and annex thereto a summons directed to the

Sheriff or his Deputy, of the county wherein the
town to be summoned is, in substance as follows :

————, *ss.*

(Seal.) *To the Sheriff of the county of*   *or his*
        Deputy,

                        GREETING.

Justice's sum- IN the name of the Commonwealth of *Massachu-*
mons.   *setts,* you are hereby required to summons the town of   in the said
county of   to appear if they see
fit, before me the subscriber, a Justice of the Peace,
in and for said county of   on   the   day
of   at   of the clock in the   noon, to shew
cause, if any they have, why the prayer of the above
written complaint should not be granted, by leaving
an attested copy thereof, and of this summons, with
the Overseers of the said town of   or some one
of them, thirty days before said   day of
and make return hereof, and of your doings herein,
unto me the said Justice, on or before the said
day of   Hereof fail not.
    Given under my hand and seal the   day of
in the year of our Lord   T. F.
    And such officer shall serve and return the same,
his being an inhabitant of the town to be summoned
notwithstanding, for the same fees, as for other writs
Party and wit- of summons. And such Justice shall
nesses to be summon the party to be removed, and
summoned. other witnesses, and may, if he see
cause, compel the appearance of the former by warrant, to be examined ; and shall hear
his objections to such removal, and may for good
cause continue the process once, not exceeding three
months ; and after due examination and hearing,
whether the town summoned appears or not, shall
proceed to give judgment for, or against the complainants, and make a record thereof in substance
as follows :

—— ss.

AT a Court held before me   Esq.   Form of judg-
a Justice of the Peace, in and for the   ment.
county of   at   in said county, on
the   day of   in the year of our Lord one
thousand seven hundred and   the town of
in the county of   complains against the town of
    in the county of *   shewing that   now
resident in said town of *   is poor   and become
chargeable to that town (or is likely to become
chargeable, as the fact may be) and that said
town of   is the place of his lawful settlement,
and praying it may be so adjudged, and that he may
be removed thither (and for damages for expenses
incurred on account of such pauper, or that may be
incurred, and for costs :) The parties appear (or the
complainants appear, but the said town of   although solemnly called, doth not appear, but makes
default, as the case may be) and after due examination and hearing, and on due consideration of the
premises had, I do adjudge the same to be true, and
I do also adjudge that the lawful settlement of the
said   is in the said town of   . and that he be
removed thither, and that the complainants recover
costs (or that the complainants recover the sum of
    damages, for expenses incurred to this time
for the support of the said   as the case may require)(or if in favor of the town complained of, say,
I do adjudge that the said   is not likely to become
chargeable to said town of   or that the lawful
settlement of said   is not in said town of
and that said town of   recover costs.)

        Recorded by me,

                Justice of the Peace.

    No costs, however, to be awarded for   Costs may be
such town if defaulted ; but if the com-   awarded as
plaint be not entered or be discontinu-   the case may
ed, or not prosecuted, the town com-   be.

plained of appearing, and praying therefor, shall recover costs. And upon judgment of removal, such
Justice may issue his warrant of removal, directed
to, and to be executed by any Constable of the
town from whence the person is to be removed, or
to any particular person by name in the following
form :

(Seal.) S————ss.

To any constable in the town of   in the
county of   or to

GREETING.

WHEREAS at a Court held on   before me

Warrant of removal.   Esq. a Justice of the Peace, in and
for the county of   on the   day of
it was adjudged by me the said Jus-
tice, that   now resident in said town of   is
chargeable (or likely to become chargeable, as the
case may be) thereto ; that his lawful settlement is
in the town of   in the county of   and that he
be removed thither. I do therefore, in the name
of the Commonwealth of *Massachusetts*, hereby au-
thorise and require you forthwith to take, remove
and convey, by land or water, as may be most convenient, the said   to the town of   and him
deliver to the Overseers of the poor thereof, or some
one of them, who are hereby required to receive
and provide for him, as an inhabitant of that town.
And of this warrant and of your doings herein, you
are to make return to me, as soon as may be, after
you shall have executed the same.

Given under my hand and seal the   day of
in the year of our Lord one thousand seven
hundred and

Justice of the Peace,

And such Overseers shall be obliged to receive

Overseers to provide.   and provide for such person accordingly ; and said Justice may also award ex-
ecution for damages and costs ; and may

tax in costs a reasonable sum for the expense of removal; and the execution may be issued to, and may be executed by a proper officer, in the county where the town is, against which it issues. And in all the proceedings aforesaid, the word *district* shall be inserted instead of the word *town*, where the cases require it.

Execution may be issued against the town.

12. *Provided always*, That either party, as also any person who shall be adjudged likely to become chargeable and ordered to be removed, aggrieved at the judgment of such Justice, may appeal therefrom to the next Court of Common Pleas, to be holden in and for the same county, and shall produce copies, and enter and prosecute the same as other appeals are. And said Court shall hear and determine the same without a Jury, and may award like warrant for removal, and like execution for damages and costs, *mutatis mutandis ;* or may on complaint affirm the judgment of the Justice with additional damages and costs, where the appeal is not prosecuted, and carry such judgment into execution.

Proviso.

13. *And be it further enacted*, That such complaint may be originally made by said overseers, if they see fit, to the Court of Common Pleas in their county, by filing the same with the Clerk of said Court, and procuring a like summons from him, *mutatis mutandis,* and causing the same to be served in time and manner as aforesaid, as also summons for the party to be removed, and for witnesses ; and such Court, upon such complaint, shall proceed to hear, determine, adjudge and grant warrant and execution, in the same manner as in cases coming before them by appeal ; and in all their adjudications in the premises, they shall state the facts upon which their

Complaints to be made by Overseers.

Court of Common Pleas to hear and determine.

Parties may appeal. judgments are founded, to the end that error therein, if any, may be corrected by writ of error, in the Supreme Judicial Court, to which either party aggrieved shall be entitled, if purchased within a year, but not otherwise, and upon which, if judgment be reversed, such judgment shall be given, as ought to have been given below, and the plaintiffs in error shall be restored to all they lost by such erroneous judgment, with costs ; but if the judgment be affirmed, the defendants shall recover costs. And said Supreme Judicial Court may send to said Court of Common Pleas, and require them to state other facts, when it shall appear by suggestion or otherwise, that some material ones were omitted in the statement aforesaid, or to explain such as do not appear to the Court to be clearly stated ; unless a new statement be agreed to by the parties. And depositions may be used before the Justice as well as Court of Common Pleas, on the trial of such complaints, when taken legally and for legal cause. And when expenses for support of a pauper are prayed for in such complaint, the same complaint may be proceeded upon to judgment so far as respects his settlement, and such expenses ; the decease of the pauper pending the complaint notwithstanding. But all complaints

Complaints—where to be prosecuted. and suits for removal of paupers, or recovery of expenses for their support to be made and prosecuted by the town of *Boston*, in the county of *Suffolk*, shall be made and prosecuted either in the county of *Middlesex* or *Norfolk*, and all such suits and complaints to be made and prosecuted by the town of *Sherburne*, in the county of *Nantucket*, or by any town in the county of *Duke's County*, shall be made and prosecuted either in the county of *Bristol* or *Barnstable*.

14. *Provided always, and be it further enacted,* That
Proviso. said Overseers may in all cases, if they

judge it expedient, previous to any such application to any Justice of the Peace, or Court of Common Pleas, send a written notification, stating the facts relating to any person actually become chargeable to their town or district, to one or more of the Overseers of the place where his settlement is supposed to be, and requesting them to remove him, which they shall have power to do by a written order directed to any particular person by name, who is hereby authorised and required to obey the same ; and if such removal is not effected, nor objected to by them in writing, after such notice, to be delivered in writing within two months after such notice to the Overseers of the town or district, requesting such removal, or to some one of them, then such Overseers may remove such person by land or water, as is most convenient, by a written order directed to and to be served by any person who shall be particularly mentioned in such order, to said place of his supposed settlement, the Overseers whereof shall be obliged to receive and provide for him, and their town or district shall be liable for the expenses of his support and removal, to be recovered by action, as aforesaid, by the town or district incurring the same, and shall be barred from contesting the question of settlement with the plaintiffs in such action. And if any person lawfully removed, agreeably to this act, to the place of his lawful settlement within this Commonwealth, shall voluntarily return to the town or district from which he was removed without their consent, he shall be deemed a vagabond, and upon conviction thereof, before any Justice of the Peace in the same county, may be sent to the house of correction.

15. *And be it further enacted*, That said Overseers shall also relieve and support, and in case of their decease, decently bury all poor persons residing or found in their

Overseers to order burials.

G

R. Newton

towns or districts, having no lawful settlements within this Commonwealth, when they stand in need, and may employ them as other paupers may be ; the expense whereof may be recovered of their relations, if they have any chargeable by law for their support, in manner herein before pointed out ; otherwise it shall be paid out of the Treasury of the Commonwealth by warrant from the Governor, by and with advice of Council, an account thereof having been first exhibited to, and examined and allowed by the General Court. And upon complaint of such Overseers, any Justice of the Peace in their county, may by warrant directed to, and which may be executed by any Constable of their town or district, or any particular person by name, cause such pauper to be sent and conveyed by land or water, to any other State, or to any place beyond sea, where he belongs, if the Justice thinks proper, if he may be conveniently removed, at the expense of the Commonwealth ; but if he cannot be so removed, he may be sent to and relieved, and employed in the house of correction, or work house, at the public expense. And every town and district shall be holden to pay any expense which shall be necessarily incurred for the relief of any pauper, by any inhabitant not liable by law for his or her support, after notice and request made to the Overseers of the said town or district, and until provision shall be made by them.

Justices on complaint to cause pauper to be removed.

16. *And be it further enacted,* That in all actions and prosecutions by complaint founded on this act, for or against any town or district, or against any individual, the Overseers of the poor thereof, or any person by writing under their hands appointed, shall and may appear, prosecute or defend the same to final judg-

Overseers empowered to prosecute and defend, in behalf of towns.

ment and execution, in behalf of such town or district, and every act or thing required or authorised by them to be done by this act, may be done by them or the major part of them.

17. *And be it further enacted,* That if any person shall bring and leave any poor and indigent person in any town or district in this Commonwealth, wherein such pauper is not lawfully settled, knowing him to be poor and indigent, he shall forfeit and pay the sum of *twenty pounds* for every such offence, to be sued for and recovered by, and to the use of such town or district by action of debt, in any Court proper to try the same.

Forfeiture in case.

18. *And be it further enacted,* That if any master or other person, having charge of any vessel, shall therein bring into, and land, or suffer to be landed in any place within this Commonwealth, any person, before that time convicted in any other State, or in any foreign country, of any infamous crime, or any for which he hath been sentenced to transportation, knowing of such conviction, or having reason to suspect it, or any person of a notoriously dissolute, infamous and abandoned life and character, knowing him or her to be such, shall for every such offence forfeit the sum of *one hundred pounds*, one half thereof to the use of the Commonwealth, and the other half to the use of any person, being a citizen of, and residing in this Commonwealth, who shall prosecute and sue for the same, by action of debt as aforesaid.

Masters of vessels prohibited from bringing in infamous persons.

And in order to prevent charge to the Commonwealth, or any towns or districts therein, by the importation of such convicts, or of infirm and vicious persons,

19. *Be it further enacted,* That the master or any other person, having charge of any vessel arriving

On entry, to make report of passengers. at any place within this Commonwealth, with any passengers on board from any foreign dominion or country, without the United States of America, shall within forty eight hours after such arrival, make a report in writing under his hand of all such passengers, their names, nation, age, character and condition, so far as hath come to his knowledge, to the Overseers of the poor of the town or district, at, or nearest to which such vessel shall arrive, who shall record the same in a book kept for that purpose in their office. And every such master or other person, that shall neglect to make such report, or that shall wittingly and willingly make a false one, shall, for each of these offences, forfeit the sum of *fifty pounds*, to be sued for and recovered by action of debt as afore-said, by, and to the use of such town or district.

20. *And be it further enacted by the authority afore-said,* That an act, entitled " An Act providing for the support of the poor," passed the fourteenth day of *February*, in the year of our Lord one thousand seven hundred and eighty nine, and all other laws, and parts of laws heretofore made and passed, relative to the support, employ-ment, binding, warning out or removal of the poor, be, and the same hereby are repealed ; saving that they shall remain in force as to all ac-tions or prosecutions already commenc-ed and now pending upon them ; saving also, that all acts and things already lawfully done and com-pleted, under and by force of them, be, and hereby are confirmed and declared to be valid ; and saving further, that this repeal shall not be construed to extend to an act, entitled " An Act for suppressing and punishing of rogues, vagabonds, common beg-gars, and other idle, disorderly and lewd persons," passed the twenty sixth day of *March*, in the year of our Lord one thousand seven hundred and eighty

Acts repealed.

Exceptions.

eight ; nor to an act, entitled, " An Act for erect-ing work houses for the reception and employment of the idle and indigent," passed the tenth day of *January*, in the year of our Lord, one thousand seven hundred and eighty nine ; nor to an act passed the present session of the General Court, entitled, " An Act ascertaining what shall constitute a legal settlement of any person, in any town or district within this Commonwealth, so as to entitle him to support therein, in case he becomes poor and stands in need of relief, and for repealing all laws hereto-fore made respecting such settlement."

This Act relates chiefly to the support, employ-ment and removal of paupers. It however contains some important provisions respecting their settle-ment. It provides three methods by which their place of settlement may be determined, or by which a town may be estopped from contesting the ques-tion of settlement in regard to a person alledged to belong to such town.

1. By judgment upon a *complaint* filed before a Justice of the Peace, or a Court of Common Pleas.

2. By judgment *in an action* for the maintenance of a pauper, against the town, in which his settle-ment is alledged in the Writ.

3. Where a town, having been at expense in sup-porting a pauper, gives notice in writing to the town where his settlement is supposed to be, stating the facts relating to the pauper, and requesting his re-moval ; and the town notified does not, within two months after notice, remove the pauper, nor object thereto in writing ; and then the town which gave notice actually removes the pauper to the town no-tified, and brings an action to recover the expenses of his support and removal : in such case the town notified is barred or estopped from contesting the question of settlement with the plaintiffs in the ac-tion.

A determination in either of these ways is conclusive between the towns who are parties to the question and between them only.

The method of estoppel last mentioned may take effect in cases where the pauper is not in fact removed.

In an action against a town for expenses incurred in the support and *burial* of a pauper, the defendants are barred from contesting the settlement of the pauper, if the Overseers have neglected for two months after notice and request, to remove him, and no objection has been made to such request.— 1 *Mass. T. Rep.* 518 & 463.

Also there may be cases where regular notice is given by one town to another, and no objection is made in two months by the town notified, and yet the latter is not barred from contesting the question of settlement with the former.

If the town of A. has incurred expense in the support of a pauper supposed to have his legal settlement in B. and the Overseers of A. give notice thereof to the Overseers of B. and request his removal, although the notice be not answered nor objected to, and the expenses are paid by the town of B. but the pauper is not removed, in an action against the town of B. for after expenses incurred by the town of A. in the support of the pauper, the defendants are not concluded from denying that the settlement of the pauper is in B.—4 *Mass Rep.* 180.

If when the removal was not objected to in two months, the plaintiffs had in fact removed the pauper, the defendants could not then have denied the settlement of the pauper to be in their town.   Or if the plaintiffs had not removed the pauper, but had, without or after the removal, commenced an action against the defendants to recover the expenses of supporting the pauper, and had recovered judgment, this judgment would have concluded the defendants.—*Ibid.*

The opinion of the Court in the case of Bridge-water against Dartmouth, goes to explain the doc-trine of estoppels, as applied to questions of settle-ment.

" *PARSONS, C. J.* The action is *assumpsit*, in which the plaintiffs demand of the defendants the sum of 242 dollars 27 cents for the maintenance of *Jane Wing*, and her three children, *John*, *Cassandra*, and *Priscella*, and for the funeral expenses of *John*, between the months of July, 1804, and November, 1805 : and also a further sum of 20 dollars for the maintenance and funeral expences of *Hannah Slocum*, alledging that they were all paupers, whose settle-ments were in *Dartmouth*.

Upon the general issue pleaded, a verdict was found for the plaintiffs, for the two sums, by the consent of the parties, subject to the opinion of the Court on certain facts agreed by them.

In looking into the case, there is no evidence that the settlement of any of the paupers was in *Dart-mouth* : the plaintiffs claim a verdict on the ground that the defendants are estopped to deny the settle-ment to be in their town.

It appears that neither of these towns choose O-verseers of the poor, but the Selectmen act in that character : that in June, 1802, *Jane Wing* and her three children having been maintained by *Bridge-water*, the Selectmen of that town gave notice to the Selectmen of *Dartmouth*, with a bill of the ex-pences, agreeably to the twelfth section of the stat-ute of 1793, c. 59, and requested them to remove the paupers. The Selectmen of *Dartmouth* did not return any answer to this notice, but paid the bill ; and the paupers were not removed from *Bridgewa-ter*. On the 27th of August, 1804, after a portion of the expenses demanded in this action had been incurred by the plaintiffs, the Selectmen of *Bridge-*

water again notified the Selectmen of *Dartmouth*, that two of *Jane Wing's* children were chargeable for their support, and requested the Selectmen of *Dartmouth* to remove them. To this notice an answer was returned on the 20th of October following, purporting to be from the Selectmen of *Dartmouth*, but signed by one of them only, denying the settlement of *Jane Wing* or her children to be in *Dartmouth*.

The plaintiffs have urged that as the Selectmen of *Dartmouth* did not object to the first notice, but paid the bill of expenses, the defendants are estopped as to *Bridgewater* to deny the settlement to be in *Dartmouth*, and especially as the objection to the second notice is signed only by one of the Selectmen.

It is well settled that estoppels, by which a party is prevented from defending himself by telling the truth, are to be confined within strict rules. And we are of opinion that the statute of 1793, c. 59, provides estoppels but in three cases.

One case is where notice has been given pursuant to the 12th section of that statute, and (no objection being made within two months) the town giving the notice have actually removed the paupers to the town, to which notice was regularly given. This is not the present case; for *Bridgewater* did not in fact remove the paupers to *Dartmouth*.

Another case of estoppel is, when a town has recovered judgment against another town for the maintenance or removal of a pauper alledged to belong to the last town; such judgment is conclusive between the parties, as to all future charges of maintenance. Neither is this the present case; for *Dartmouth* paid the bill without a suit.

The plaintiffs failing on these grounds have further insisted that no objection was made in two months by the Selectmen of *Dartmouth* to the second notice, which is the foundation of this action. If this appear from the facts agreed, this is the third case, in which the defendants are estopped to contest a settlement. The objection is drawn up, as the language of all the Selectmen, in the plural number, and against the name of the subscriber is written " Selectmen of *Dartmouth*." This we consider as a subscription in behalf of the Selectmen. The statute requires the objection to be in writing ; but does not require it to be signed by the greater number of the Selectmen : and the defendants in this action consider the written objection as the act of their Selectmen. We are therefore of opinion that the defendants are not estopped from disputing the settlement on the ground that their Selectmen did not object within two months. Indeed the second notice is very imperfect. It has no relation to *Jane ;* but is confined wholly to two of her children, without naming them.

The defendants not being estopped, the plaintiffs cannot recover any thing for the maintenance of *Jane Wing* and her children, or for the funeral expenses of her son *John*.

The demand of 20 dollars for the maintenance and funeral expenses of *Hannah Slocum* stands on a different foundation. The Selectmen of *Bridgewater* gave regular notice to the Selectmen of *Dartmouth* and requested her removal. To this no answer was returned, and the defendants are in this action estopped to deny that her settlement was in *Dartmouth*.—*4 Mass. Rep.* 273.

In the case of Quincy against Braintree, the former gave notice to the latter in writing as follows .

" *Quincy*, October 7, 1807.

" GENTLEMEN,

" The widow *Hannah White*, an inhabitant of " your town, is now in our care, and we conceive

H

" it necessary to give you this information, that you
" may order her removal as soon as possible. The
" said *Hannah* has been boarded at an expense of one
" dollar and twenty five cents per week for three
" months past, and her expenses will now be more,
" which we shall continue to charge to your town.
" We are, with much respect, gentlemen, your hum-
" ble servants,
 " By order of the Overseers of the poor of *Quincy*,
    " *Noah Curtis*, Chairman.
 " The gentlemen Selectmen or Overseers of the
" town of *Braintree*."

Two objections were made to the sufficiency of
this notice.
 1. That it was not subscribed by the Overseers of
the poor, but by one only.
 2. That there is no fact stated in the notice from
which the defendants should conclude themselves
liable to the support of the pauper.
 The opinion of the Court was delivered as follows, by
 " *SEDGWICK, J.* The only question, which a-
rises in this cause, is on the sufficiency of the notice
given by the Overseers of the poor of *Quincy* to the
Overseers of the poor of *Braintree ;* no answer having been made to it by the latter. If it be such notice as to comply with the intentions of the statute,
there is no question but that the defendants are concluded by it, and that judgment must be rendered
against them.
 Two objections are made to its sufficiency ; 1st.
that it has not the signature of a majority of the O-
verseers of *Quincy ;* but was signed by their chair-
man only. Without determining whether this objection could under any circumstances prevail, it is
a sufficient answer in this case that it is expressly a-
greed that this notice was given " by the Overseers
of *Quincy*."

The 2d objection is that the statute requires that in giving such notice as shall conclude the defendant town, the facts should be stated therein ; by which, it is said, must be intended more than is contained in this notice.

In the case of an appeal from an adjudication of the Court of Common Pleas to this Court, the statute requires all the material facts to be stated ; and it is necessary, for otherwise this Court would not have the competent means of determining whether the adjudication was correct. In that case all the material facts must be stated, which are necessary to attain the object, for which they are to be stated : and to the same effect, in relation to its purpose, must be the notice in this case.

We cannot however perceive that all such facts are not stated in this case. Those facts are, that the pauper has her settlement in *Braintree ;* that she was at the time of the notice resident in *Quincy ;* that she required support, and that it had been afforded her by the Overseers of that town. To require, as it was said the law intended, that the notice should contain an allegation of the means by which the settlement was obtained could, on the one hand, answer no purpose of utility, and might, on the other, be inconvenient and productive of embarrassment."—*5 Mass. Rep.* 86.

Estoppels are not to be favoured, because the truth may be excluded. And no party ought to be precluded from making a defence according to the truth of his own case, unless in consequence of some positive and unequivocal principle of law.—*4 Mass. Rep.* 180.

Kindred, in the degree of father and grandfather, mother and grandmother, children or grand children, by consanguinity, living within the Common-wealth, of sufficient ability, are liable by law to support each other, in proportion to their ability.

The kindred of a pauper cannot be called upon to contribute to his support but by the Overseers of the town where he has his legal settlement, or by some other of his kindred. When the Overseers of any town in which the pauper is not settled shall provide for his relief, when fallen into distress, their *only remedy*, for compensation, is against the town in which the pauper is settled, and not against any of his kindred. In such an action the declaration must aver the settlement and notice to the town liable within three months from the commencement of the expenses.—3 *Mass. Rep.* 436.

Notice to a town must be in writing. One town cannot give legal notice to another by word of mouth.

A town in which a prison is situate, is held to support a pauper confined in prison for debt, whether he has a legal settlement in any other place or not, after due application to the Overseers.—2 *Mass. Rep.* 548. & 564.

The town in which a jail is situated is liable to the jailor for the support of a poor prisoner confined for not obeying the order of the Common Pleas in providing for the maintenance of a bastard child, of which he is adjudged the putative father ; and such town has its remedy over upon the town wherein the prisoner has his settlement, or if he has no settlement, upon the Commonwealth.—5 *Mass. Rep.* 244.

In a prosecution against a town for the support of a person alleged to be a pauper, it is competent to the defendants to prove his ability to maintain himself. A plea in bar stating that fact would be good on a general demurrer. Otherwise on a special demurrer, assigning for cause that it amounted to the general issue.—1 *Mass. T. Rep.* 459.

How much property a man must have in order to be able, in contemplation of law, to support himself, may perhaps be a question. In some circumstances he may have considerable property and still be a pauper. This seems to follow as a consequence of an Act passed the 13th of March, 1806.

An Act to exempt certain Goods and Chattels of Debtors from Attachment and Execution.

" SECT. 1. *Be it enacted by the Senate and House of Representatives, in General Court assembled, and by the authority of the same,* That from and after the first day of *May* next, the wearing apparel, beds, bedsteads, bedding, and household utensils of any debtor, necessary for himself, his wife, and children, the tools of any debtor, necessary for his trade or occupation, the bibles and school books which may be in actual use in his or her family, together with one cow and one swine, shall be altogether exempted from attachment and execution ; and no civil officer shall attach, levy upon, or take the same, or any part thereof, either upon mesne process or execution.—*Provided neverthelefs,* That the beds and bedding exempted as aforesaid, shall not exceed one bed, bedstead, and necessary bedding to two persons, and household furniture the value of *fifty dollars,* upon any just apprisement.

SECT. 2. *Be it further enacted,* That no debtor or debtors, owning any of the goods and chattels aforesaid, shall be thereby precluded from the benefit of an Act, passed the nineteenth day of *November,* in the year of our Lord one thousand seven hundred and eighty-seven, entitled, " An Act for the relief of poor prisoners who are committed by execution for debt," and instead of the oath or affirmation thereby prescribed to be taken, whenever the Justices, thereby authorized to administer an oath or affirmation, shall think proper to administer such oath or affirmation, there shall be taken an oath or affirmation in form following, to wit :—I do solemnly swear, before Almighty God, (or affirm, as the case may be,) that I have not any estate, real or personal, in possession, reversion, or remainder, sufficient to support myself in prison, or to pay prison charges ; except the goods and chattels exempted from attachment and execution, by an Act, entitled, " An Act to exempt certain goods and chattels of debtors from attachment and execution ;" and that I have not, since the commencement of this suit against me, or at any other time, directly or indirectly, sold, leased, or otherwise conveyed, or disposed of to, or entrusted any person or persons whomsoever, with all or any part of the estate, real or personal, whereof I have been the lawful owner or possessor, with any intent or design to secure the same, or to receive or to expect any profit or advantage therefor ; or have caused or suffered to be done, any thing else whatsoever, whereby any of my creditors may be defrauded. So help me God ; or (this I do under the pains and penalties of perjury) as the case may be."

According to this Act, a man committed to jail for debt may lawfully swear out unless he has property enough to support himself in prison besides what is exempted as aforesaid. And if he may lawfully swear out, it is presumed the town in which the jail is situate is liable for his support while thus imprisoned, and may have its remedy over against the town in which the prisoner has a legal settlement.

During the periods before mentioned, provision was made from time to time, for the purpose of securing towns against the charges to which they were and might be exposed in various ways ; as by the manumission of slaves, and the bringing of paupers into towns and leaving them there by masters of vessels and others. These provisions may be seen by having recurrence to the aforesaid statutes of the 4 Will. and Mar. and the 12 and 13 Will. 3—the 2 Anne, paſſed in 1703—the 4 and 5 Geo. 2, publiſhed Nov. 10th, 1731—the 10 Geo. 2, paſſed in 1736—and the aforesaid Acts, of 1739 and 26th of Feb. 1794.

Towns sometimes have occasion to make application to the General Court to obtain payment for expenses which have accrued for supporting persons who are the proper poor of the State. The manner in which such application is to be made, the facts necessary to be therein stated, and the evidence necessary to accompany it, are particularly pointed out in the following Act, passed the 26th of Feb. 1799.

An Act specifying the Evidence to accompany Accounts exhibited for the Support of the Poor of the Commonwealth.

" SECT. 1. *Be it enacted by the Senate and House of Representatives, in General Court assembled, and by the authority of the same,* That the Selectmen or Overseers of the Poor in the several towns and districts within this Commonwealth, when they shall make application to the General Court for payment of any expenses which may have accrued for supporting any poor person, shall be required to make and exhibit a certificate, setting forth the place from whence such person came, the time of his or her coming into this Commonwealth, and where he or she shall have resided subsequent to his or her coming into the same, and that he or she has not gained a settlement in any town or district within the Commonwealth in any of the ways pointed out in an Act passed *February* eleventh, in the year of our Lord seventeen hundred and ninety-four, specifying what shall constitute a legal settlement : And also, that he or she has no kindred within the Commonwealth by law obliged to support him or her. And in case such person came into this Commonwealth before the tenth day of *April*, in the year of our Lord seventeen hundred and sixty-six, whether he or she was warned according to law to depart from the town or district wherein he or she resided. And if such application be for payment of expenses incurred for the support of a woman who shall have married a person not an inhabitant of this Commonwealth, or for the child of such woman ; then the said Selectmen or Overseers shall be required to certify, that such woman or child has no legal settlement in any place in this Commonwealth, according to the existing laws for determining questions of habitancy ; in all which certificates the said Selectmen or Overseers shall certify, that they make the same on the best evidence they can obtain.

SECT. 2. *Be it further enacted*, That a Resolve passed the twenty-ninth day of *February*, in the year of our Lord one thousand seven hundred and ninety-six, establishing the evidence to accompany accounts exhibited for the support of the State poor, be and hereby is repealed."